The Red Knight

Written by Lisa Thompson
Pictures by Andy Hamilton

The red Knight had a red suit.

"Look at my shiny, red suit!"

The red Knight had a red horse.

"Look at my big, red horse!"

The red Knight liked to eat red jelly.

"Red jelly is the best for a red Knight."

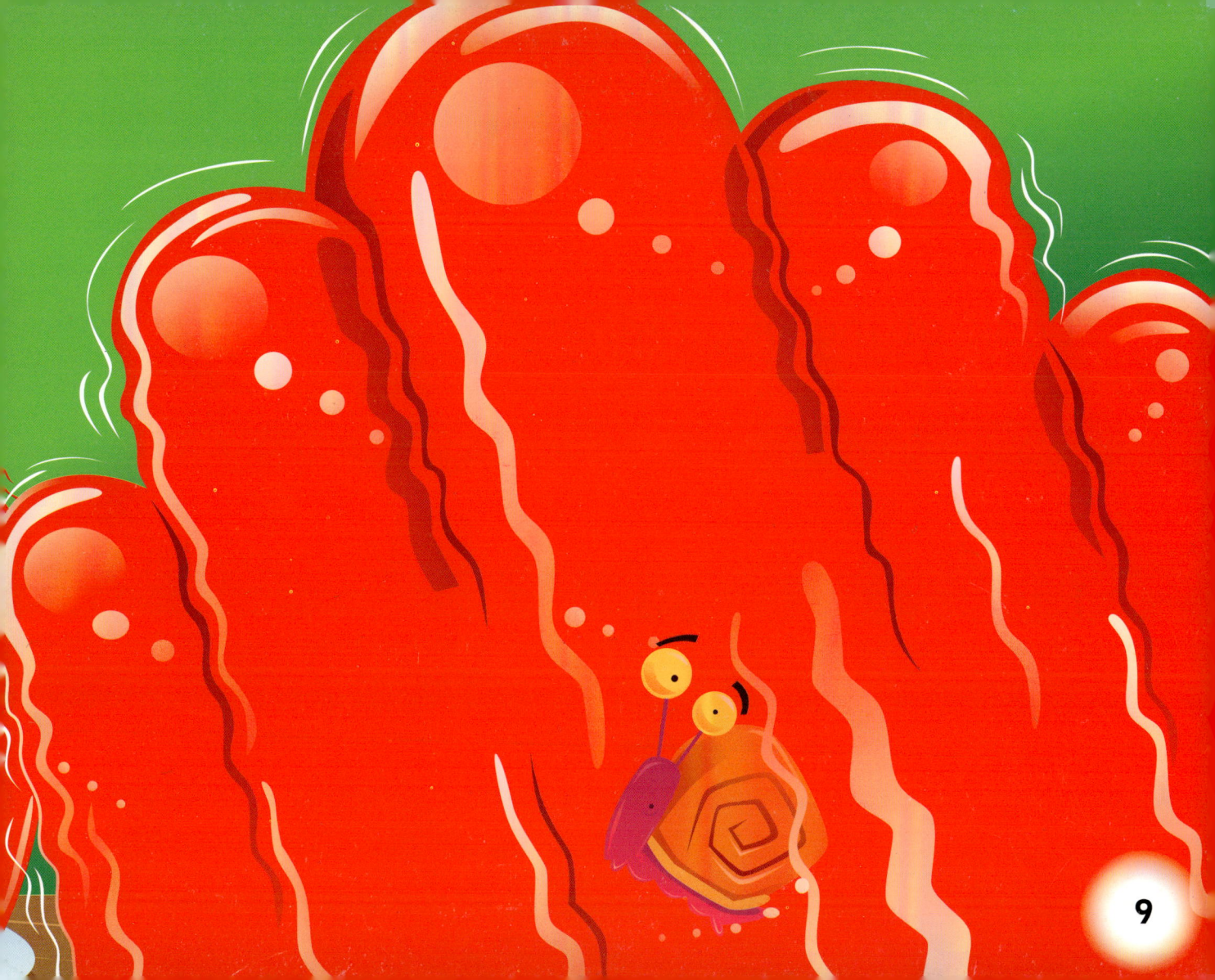

The red Knight lived in a red castle.

"Look at my big, red castle!"

"Look at my tall, red tower.
I like to look down from my red tower."